notes

from the first year

MILES HOWARD

To Nick
(and everyone else at Bigfoot West that shitty night)

CONTENTS

Introduction

It's the first day of the year 2018.

The President of the United States is an authoritarian conman with a history of racism and self-congratulatory tales of sexual assault. His party is led by extremists whose political careers have been financed by corporations and oligarchs, and whose views on taxation, social welfare, environmental protections, guns, religion, civil rights, and money in politics are not shared by a majority of the American people. These men and women are in power largely thanks to partisan redistricting measures and new voter eligibility requirements that have given some communities a disproportionately strong influence in elections while suppressing the votes of many others. They are also in power because the opposition party—the party best positioned to resist and overthrow the regime—has lost its stomach for fighting ruthlessly, as well as its ambition to build a better country than the one in which millions of Americans have been struggling to survive.

None of this should be a shock to anyone. But that doesn't make it any less alarming.

The American stage has long been set for a crisis like this. Soaring and unchecked rates of income inequality and poverty, a steady decline in the availability of jobs and the value of the minimum wage, long-ignored undercurrents of socially palatable misogyny and bigotry, and our ongoing refusal to reckon with the limits of a "free market" society are among the many forces that have contributed to a destabilized climate in which a white collar gangster like Donald Trump could run for president—masquerading as a populist while scapegoating brown people and feminists as America's problem. The moment the Republican Party leadership threw its weight behind Trump at the 2016 Republican National Convention was when the endgame became crystal clear. If the GOP's historically unpopular agenda of handouts for the wealthy and bootstrapper austerity for everyone else was the kerosene-soaked rag, Trump was the match that could spark an inferno that would engulf the nation while most

Americans were busy laughing at the clown in the Oval Office or wishing for him to be devoured by wild pigs.

That's what happened in 2017.

Today, Donald Trump is fat and angry in the White House while the Republican Congress sharpens its knives and gazes at Medicare, Medicaid, and Social Security with a wolf-like grin. The events that brought America to this precipice have been thoroughly documented by journalists, authors, academics, legal experts, and political science majors. Not so long from now, this mass documentation will serve as testimony for one of the weirdest and most consequential chapters of the American Democratic Experiment. It will offer our kids a window into what many of us were thinking, saying, and doing as one giant asshole, his political servants, and their donors had their way with the rest of us.

But for the near-term future, this coverage of modern America exists as a narrative trail: for the fights and challenges from which we cannot afford to divert our attention or our emotions.

Which brings us to the story of how and why I joined this effort. Of how this book came to be.

Like many others, I didn't plan to spend 2017 writing about the comings and goings of U.S. politics. When the 2015 Republican primaries began, I was a 27 year-old "young professional" trying to cut it as a writer. 11 months of covering nightlife and movies at the Boston Phoenix and several years of sporadic freelancing—during which I wrote about college programs, autumnal shopping destinations, and at one point, organic penis enlargement cream—taught me how to write about almost anything. But I lacked focus: I craved something substantive that I could consistently sink my editorial teeth into. Between 2013 and 2015, I had spent some time traveling around the United States to talk with Millennial-aged young people about the economy, their life prospects, and the upcoming U.S. election cycle. It was a pet project inspired by Studs Terkel's *Working*. I tried to score a publishing deal for a collection of these interviews, but none of the agents or publishers I queried saw a market for the book: especially since I was a new author and not a nationally-recognized expert on the trials and tribulations of Millennials. In 2016, after getting laid off from a healthcare startup that had recruited me as a "content strategist," I knew it was time to make a big change.

The week before Donald Trump became president-elect, I moved from Boston to L.A. to pursue a career in screenwriting. Since the age of 17, I had casually written horror and sci-fi scripts in the vein of *Dawn of the Dead* and *The Thing*. I went west because I wanted to make a modest pile of cash optioning and selling those screenplays. (Horror movies are cheap to make and usually do well on opening weekend, so this is an ideal genre for a new writer to crack into.) I lived in L.A. for four years as a college student. I also knew people in Hollywood, including agency staffers, who might look at my treatments. Going to L.A., playing the networking and social climbing game, and trying to get signed with CAA, Gersh, or William Morris was one of those, "Fuck it, why not?" life decisions. There was probably never going to be an easier time to take a shot at this. So I packed my life into two duffel bags, moved in with a college classmate of mine at a creaky but character-rich house in the neighborhood known as West Adams, and began dusting off my scripts.

On the night of November 8th, 2016, I took the Metro to Palms to hang out with a friend of mine. We had met as student newspaper writers back in 2010 and since then, we had talked regularly about the state of politics in the U.S. Our plan was to watch the presidential election coverage at a western-themed bar that had cheap whiskey. When I arrived at my friend's apartment to meet him, the major networks were already calling the election results in east coast states. As I waited for my friend to grab his jacket, I scrolled through my phone's newsfeed and noticed that Donald Trump had just won Virginia. *Huh*, I remember thinking. *That wasn't supposed to happen.* My friend emerged from his room and we headed out to the bar.

Nearly six hours later—well after midnight—the two of us stumbled back into the apartment hammered, quietly horrified by what had just happened to America, and not quite sure what to say to each other. I collapsed on the couch and fell into the darkest slumber before jerking awake just an hour later to go and puke in my friend's toilet. I remember, in the morning, hugging my friend for what felt like several minutes before beginning the journey back to my neighborhood.

It was a broiling day, even by SoCal standards, and the streets were nearly empty. This was spookier than anything I had ever experienced in L.A.—a city infamous for its endless rivers of fenders and brakelights. By the time I unlocked the front door of my house, I had called and spoken with my parents, my sister, and a few friends. (The LA Metro is affordable, if not particularly speedy.) I took a shower and slept through most of the day. When I got up, it was dark outside. I decided to go see a new movie, *Arrival,* in order to take my mind off the implications of the election for a few hours.

But midway to the theater, sitting near the back of the 754 bus, I found myself overwhelmed by a single, terrifying thought. *Are my mom and dad going to lose their Medicare benefits?* I knew that Paul Ryan and many of the Republican Senators and Representatives wanted to bleed this program dry. With Trump heading for the White House and a GOP majority for Congress, there was nothing to stand in their way. If Medicare collapsed, both my mother and father would likely find themselves in a terrible place if either of them suddenly became ill or suffered an accident. This stroke of bad luck could have profound implications for our family.

We had lived comfortably, but we were not rich, by any stretch of the imagination. I couldn't stop thinking about this nightmare: not on the bus, not when I arrived at the movie theater, not when the lights went down, and not even when they came back up two hours later.

Like so many other Americans at the time, I sank rapidly into a toxic jetsam of depression and anxiety that lasted for weeks. I couldn't put a pen to paper or find the energy to attend events where one could bump shoulders and make small talk with power brokers in Hollywood. Towards the end of November, I went up to Portland to spend Thanksgiving with my cousins, aunts, and uncles, which shook me from the dark spell. The night after, as I waited in the PDX airport terminal for my flight back to L.A., I found myself looking at the departures board. I gazed longingly at various east coast destinations. New York City. Manchester. Burlington. Montreal. And of course, *Boston*.

The irony of the situation clobbered me. I had gone west to chase a dream that involved giving nightmares to moviegoers, but now I was *living* in a nightmare more tangible and consequential than anything a screenwriter could have conjured. More than any other time in my life, I was freaked out, furious, homesick (and worried) for my friends and family back east, and absurdly out of place. I didn't want to write escapist entertainment. I wanted to do something that could help reverse the grim odds we now faced.

And then, I remembered.

I had spent the past three years researching and writing a book about Millennial voters: the largest living generation in America, and the generation best positioned to defeat Trump and the GOP.

America was about to enter a period of political upheaval from which there might not be a return. There would be an urgent need for craftspeople capable of distilling all of this upheaval into narratives that ordinary folks could understand.

I could do this.

Shortly after Christmas, I moved back to Boston. I resolved to spend most of my time writing about the state of politics in the U.S.—not merely documenting the abuses of the Trump administration and the GOP Congress, but writing about the sort of ideas that many of my friends, colleagues, and the young voters I spent years interviewing wanted to see the Democratic Party adopt and rally behind. I self-published my book about Millennials—I called it *The Early Voters*—and I started using the book as an introductory credential: a reason for people to care about what I had to say. I also spent many hours becoming better educated on issues such as immigration, affordable housing initiatives, and healthcare programs. My research took me to activist chapter meetings, policy think tanks, campaigns for public office, hearings at the Massachusetts State House, and Washington D.C. I managed to find a home for my writing—including several of the essays in this book—at Boston's National Public Radio outlet, WBUR 90.9. Other stories and essays I either published myself or squirreled away for publishing at a later time. The work took me to some unexpected places, including a gubernatorial campaign that I worked for as a communications consultant, speechwriter, and Millennial whisperer. It took some time for all of this to constitute even a lean living. But by Thanksgiving of 2017, I was in a very different place than I was exactly one year ago, and much happier for it.

I had finally found something that I wanted to spend much of my life writing about.

It just has happened to be politics.

I open with this story to illustrate one of the many paths that a person can take from being a political bystander to becoming a player. While the attendant privileges, opportunities, and penchants will vary wildly for each person, the one constant that most tales of political "activation" carry is the force with which politics can assimilate a willing host. Once you let politics in, that's it. Much of what you do henceforth becomes susceptible to its influence. When your morning train gets delayed due to malfunctioning track switches, your first thought is no longer, *Why does our public transit suck so much?* Instead, you start wondering if city or state officials have dropped the ball on public transit investment. When you're in line at the supermarket and the person in front of you is being mean to the cashier, you not only think, *What a prick,* but you also consider something along the lines of, *Service workers should be paid a hell of a lot more than minimum wage for dealing with this shit!* You start to connect the dots between everyday injustices and the more unwieldy structural machinations that allow those injustices to continue afflicting our shared lives.

As we close the book on the first year of Trump and head into a new year (with elections!), I have assembled a collection of my writing that charts some of the darkest and brightest moments of 2017: a collection that constitutes my first year as a full-time political writer. The scope of these notes ranges from national to super localized, but the issues at the heart of each piece couldn't be more applicable to the civic dangers posed by Trump and his political enablers. My hope is that this book will serve as an episodic manual for those who are confused by what's happening in America right now, a light for those who are scared, an alarm bell for those who aren't paying attention to any of this stuff, and an encouraging prod for anyone else considering a career in the trenches of American politics.

It needs you now.

Seeing green

JANUARY 26, 2017

A few nights ago, the White House.org page on climate change suddenly vanished without explanation. Its absence, and the absence of any rationale for deleting the page, reminds us that Donald Trump is going treat the environment like a used car, ready to be stripped for parts. The president's recent flood of executive orders—clearing the way for the Keystone XL and Dakota Access pipeline projects, imposing an media blackout on the EPA, and tapping climate science denialist Scott Pruitt for EPA administrator—confirms what many of us have long understood: Trump and his administration will plunder the natural world and let future generations deal with the consequences.

In revealing his hand so bluntly, Trump has effectively declared war on Millennials, who will live long enough to experience the most cataclysmic damages of climate change.

This is a war that Trump will lose.

I come to this conversation having spent the last three years asking Millennial-aged adults what they care about. I began this project because I, too, am a Millennial, and I wanted to find out why so many of my peers didn't vote in the 2010 and 2014 midterms. Put another way, I wanted to know what issues Millennials might rally around in upcoming elections. So I traveled across the United States on buses, trains, and on foot, and I talked with more than 300 people in teens, twenties, and thirties.

When I began the interviews, I expected student loan debt—an immediate and tangible crisis felt by millions of young people—to emerge as the dominant issue that kept Millennials up at night. What I heard instead, in both blue and red states, was a more sobering and chilling answer: *climate change.* Roughly 80 percent of the Millennials I spoke with told me that the manifest effects of climate change and whether these effects will deprive them and their children of a habitable world, is the most pressing issue of our time.

It's not difficult to understand why climate change has emerged as the closest thing to a universal millennial nightmare. If we consider the academic definition[1] of "Millennial" as the generation comprised of those born between 1982 and 2004, then can we assume most Millennials are old enough to remember Al Gore and Davis Guggenheim's 2006 film *An Inconvenient Truth*, which made climate change a part of the national discourse. Since its theatrical release, the issue has been everywhere: in the news, in pop culture, and of course, in Washington, D.C. Just as Baby Boomers were shaped by the Cold War, so Millennials have been shaped by climate change and its attendant concerns.

So why hasn't there been a Millennial-driven climate movement? The answer, paradoxically, may be Barack Obama, a more environmentally conscious U.S. president. For the past eight years, Millennials enjoyed the relative comfort of a governing administration that demonstrated

---

[1] The 1982-2004 timeframe is derived from researchers Neil Howe and William Strauss. It's something of an industry standard for citation in articles and studies of Millennials.

interest in mitigating climate change and its fallout. President Obama's victories, including the Paris Climate Agreement and his Climate Action Plan, might not have been as bold as environmental advocacy groups would have wished. But it was near impossible to look at Obama's achievements and not feel that America was at least inching towards a future in which more visionary climate advocates like Bill McKibben and Naomi Klein[2] could play an authorial role in creating environmental policy.

Trump's unexpected victory didn't just delay that future. The first several days of Trump's rule have illuminated a plan to erase the Obama presidency, including the climate victories. The security blanket that Millennials have been wrapped in has been ripped away. But those who jeer at the existential plight of young adults forget what eventually happens when people are pushed into a corner: They fight back, tooth and nail.

In the years ahead, Millennials are going to become Trump's worst nightmare, and not just

---

[2] In her 2010 book, *This Changes Everything*, Klein argues that meaningfully addressing climate change requires moving away from extractive capitalism. A bitter pill for many Americans, including some of those who supported Barack Obama.

because Trump has given young adults further reason to resent and resist his administration. Last year, Millennials claimed the Baby Boomers' long-held title of "largest living generation in America." Over the next two years, millions of Millennials will become eligible to vote. Within a decade, today's young adults will have more voting power than any other demographic in America.

Trump will be his usual vainglorious self as he settles into the Oval Office and issues legislative decrees that could compromise the longevity of Millennials. But before long, Trump will find himself in the thick of a fight that he cannot win. There will be a backlash against his assault on the environment, and it will come from the young.

It will be *tremendous*.

Believe me.

Your kids won't be much help

MARCH 10, 2017

Like many of the young Americans who came of age during the Great Recession, I constantly worry about money. It is the governing anxiety of my life. The fiscal obligations of being a "young professional"—paying for groceries and a place to live—are daunting enough. But the questions that really make my palms sweat are far bigger in scope: Will I be able to support a family one day? Is retirement a realistic expectation for my generation? If I got cancer, could I afford the chemo? Or would I have to launch a Kickstarter campaign to subsidize my existence?

These are reasonable things for young people to be asking. Millennials—young adults born between 1982 and 2004—are inheriting an increasingly plutocratic society in which only the wealthy and connected are equipped to thrive. Decades of unmitigated wage stagnation, cost-of-living inflation, and labor automation[1] have left Millennials considerably more broke than their Baby Boomer parents and even Generation X. Among other conclusions, the U.S. Census Bureau has found that Millennials are more likely to live at home, find themselves unemployed, or slide into poverty—an existential chasm from which most never return.[2]

That was 2016.

Today, with Donald Trump installed as president, leading an administration and a Republican Congress that appears downright giddy at the prospect of eviscerating what's left of America's social welfare programs, the economic challenges facing Millennials are about to get much worse.

The intrinsic generational warfare of the GOP agenda won't come as news to anyone who has considered the implications of Trump's censorship campaign against climate change scientists, or his

---

[1] Labor automation might be the most unsung challenge facing western civilization. A recent Oxford University study suggests that a whopping 47% of U.S. workers are at risk of losing their jobs to robots between today and the year 2037.

[2] To learn more, go read Barbara Ehrenreich's *Nickel and Dimed.*

appointment of Betsy DeVos, a billionaire Christian Dominionist[3] and charter school advocate as education secretary. And now, we're on the brink of getting our first piece of legislation that will cripple the young.

That legislation is the American Health Care Act: House Republicans' long-awaited replacement for the Affordable Care Act, and a clear pathway toward record levels of youth poverty.

Taken at summary, the AHCA—or "Trumpcare," as many are calling it[4]—is a conspicuously cruel law that will hurt millions of Americans by clawing back health coverage and increasing its cost significantly. (The super rich, who don't have to worry about such things, will receive more tax cuts, of course.) By hiking the individual penalty for going uncovered from the ACA's fee of $695, or 2.5 percent of an individual's income, the Republican health care replacement is designed to intimidate Millennials into ponying up for insurance policies to avoid a lapse in coverage. Considering the Congressional Budget Office's

---

[3] This is worth noting because as a generation, Millennials are considerably less religious than older Americans.

[4] "Ryancare" would have been a more appropriate moniker. Bleeding the common good dry has been his baby for years.

projection that the AHCA would cause a surge in premium prices, the GOP bill ensures a huge handout to health insurers.

But a closer look at section 133 of Trumpcare reveals the key provision that will decimate young people and their economic standing. In lieu of the penalty that the ACA imposed upon the uninsured, the Republican replacement requires insurance companies to charge an uninsured person a cash penalty that amounts to *30 percent* of their annual premium total for the next year. This penalty would fall upon those who go without "continuous coverage" for 63 days or longer. In other words, if you were paying $500 a month for coverage and something happened—a move, job upheaval, mounting financial burdens—your penalty would be close to $2,000 for the subsequent year, on top of your regular premiums.

The fiscal rationale for imposing such outrageous penalties is simple: Millennials still aren't buying health insurance en masse. (The price tag, already insurmountable for many during the pre-Trump era, is a major deterrent.) Insurance companies need younger customers to balance the cost of covering older Americans who are more likely to get sick. But this giveaway to the insurance industry comes at the expense of an entire generation's shot at prosperity and even solvency.

There is no demographic in America at greater risk of being decimated by the continuous coverage penalties than Millennials. As many journalists and scholars have observed, Millennials change jobs and move around more than any generation in recent memory. Both of these activities carry the risk of health coverage gaps. And as we've already addressed, most Millennials aren't exactly sitting on the kind of nest egg one would need to pay an AHCA penalty without potentially life-altering hardship.

It may be tempting for Boomers and Gen X-ers to dismiss the danger that young people will face if the AHCA is signed into law, out of indifference to Millennials or resentment towards those who didn't vote for the Democrat last November. But shrugging off the vulnerability of Millennials will eventually come at a grave price for older Americans. Other than paltry social security checks, our society guarantees virtually nothing for retirees. The expenses of retirement—assisted living, in particular—must be paid for by someone else. By most accounts, the average Boomer is in no position to foot those bills independently.[5]

If the American Healthcare Act becomes law, their kids won't be much help, either.

---

[5] By most studies and estimates, the average U.S. Baby Boomer has less than $200,000 saved up for retirement.

Choose chaos

JUNE 22, 2017

Back in May, when House Republicans passed a giant tax cut for the wealthy[1] and called it the American Health Care Act of 2017, the American people responded with rage, and rightly so.

The bill was written and passed with barely any input from citizens, Democratic lawmakers, or even the Congressional Budget Office. Its most significant consequences—astronomical health premium hikes, the return of pre-existing condition discrimination and lifetime limits, deep Medicaid cuts—would kill more Americans (*far more*) than the 9/11 terror attacks.[2]

---

[1] The American Healthcare Act, as conceived and passed by the House, repealed the tax increases mandated by the Affordable Care Act, which would have resulted in a fat rebate for the rich.

[2] The 9/11 terror attacks killed 2,996 people. The Congressional Budget Office estimated that the AHCA would lead to 22 million people losing their health insurance. This, according to public health studies, would cause up to *24,000 deaths each year.*

Any assurances that the more "reasonable" Senate Republicans would rewrite and soften the odious bill before it went to the floor for a vote were swiftly shot down by Senate Majority Leader Mitch McConnell. After assembling an all-male, all-Republican working group, McConnell took the still-hot AHCA behind closed doors and barred practically anyone else from looking at the thing.

Today, Senate Republicans have unveiled a draft version of the revised AHCA, maintaining much of the House bill with modest changes to financial assistance for folks in the lower income bracket, and more severe Medicaid cuts.

As McConnell teases a pre-July 4th Senate vote for the AHCA, we now find ourselves at a perilous crossroads with little precedent in recent U.S. history. The Republican Party, in full control of our government, has rejected any measure of bipartisan discourse over a piece of legislation with life-or-death implications for millions of people.

There is only one ethical and effective way for the Democratic Party to respond to McConnell's reprehensible politics and protect the lives of its constituents and all Americans imperiled by the

AHCA. The Democrats must obstruct all Senate activity concerning the AHCA, grinding the chamber to a halt until the Republicans agree to hold public hearings on the bill. Not only is this the right thing to do, but thanks to the Indivisible group—an activist organization founded by former Congressional aides—there is now an instruction manual for doing this.

To pass the AHCA at light speed, the Republican Party has utilized a procedure called "Budget Reconciliation." This offers them the advantage of being able to pass the AHCA with only 51 votes instead of the 60 that most bills require. But there's a catch. In exchange for lowering the vote threshold, the Republicans must allow Democrats to attach amendments to the bill. And here's the best part: *there's no limit to how many amendments can be added.* This is how the Democrats can cause chaos and shut down the AHCA proceedings—file hundreds, even thousands of amendments, grind the Senate to a halt and force the Republicans to give the public a glimpse at what McConnell and his group have been doing in the shadows.

It sounds simple enough, but ironically, the

greatest obstacle to making this happen is the modern Democratic Party ethos itself. Since 2008, when McConnell notoriously declared that the Republican Party's governing mission would be denying President Obama a second term, the Democrats have positioned themselves as "civil" bipartisan peacemakers. Obama set the example himself, offering olive branch after olive branch to an increasingly immovable Republican Party.[3] It began as a noble gesture, but as the Republicans hardened, the Democrats' obsession with bipartisanship became exasperating. It begged one question: if the Republicans won't compromise on anything, what do the Democrats gain by *arriving* at the bargaining table in a compromised position?

Obama finally took the hint and spent the last two years of his second term swinging for the fences on issues such as environmental conservation, renewable energy, and a higher minimum wage. But things took a wrong turn during the 2016 election cycle, when Hillary Clinton and the Democratic leadership waged a presidential campaign aimed at courting moderate

---

[3] These compromises included softening environmental protection legislation and extending the Bush tax cuts—a decision that prompted a then-unknown Bernie Sanders to deliver an eight hour filibuster speech on the Senate floor.

Republicans instead of firing up liberals and leftists. It was a relapse, a return to the Democrats' old ways of "going high" when the other side fights dirty, and it backfired spectacularly. Even today, with the Democratic Party on life support and the Republican Party striving to shut down any semblance of Congressional dialogue on the AHCA, the Democrats' self-defeating compulsion to play nice, "get things done," and worship at the altar of bipartisanship might not be exhausted yet.

While most Democratic Senators have taken to the airwaves, Facebook, and Twitter to complain about McConnell's AHCA secrecy, not a single one has suggested holding the bill ransom with amendment filings. The optimistic way to look at this is to simply hope that the Democrats have a hardball tucked up their sleeve. But realistically, the Democrats will likely have to be pushed into this legislative knife fight by their constituents. Many will probably push back against the idea of obstructing the AHCA proceedings because it's "beneath" Senate decorum—something the Democrats like to congratulate themselves for protecting even as the Republicans piss on it.

Simply trying to resurrect Congressional

courtesy might be enough to let Democratic lawmakers sleep soundly at night. But for their constituents—most of whom lack the plump cushion of government health coverage—there are far more urgent matters that can cause insomnia.

We'll sleep better when more Democratic Senators wake up.[4]

---

[4] Spoiler: The Democrats never woke up. Their defensive measures remained polite and within the standard Senate decorum. Liberals and leftists should be ready to force their elected officials to fight ruthlessly. Visit indivisible.org for resources and call scripts when the next battle begins.

And it turns out most of us
don't want to die

JULY 20, 2017

Somewhere tonight, deep in the chambers of
Congress, Mitch McConnell is aching for a tall
glass of Kentucky bourbon.

Who could blame him?

Tuesday's resounding defeat of the Better Care
Reconciliation Act (BCRA)[1] is a legacy-staining
humiliation for the Senate majority leader, not to
mention the entire Republican Congress. After
eight years of hemming and hawing about
repealing the Affordable Care Act (ACA),
McConnell and his colleagues failed to get their act
together. Thanks to Senators Susan Collins, Rand
Paul, Mike Lee, and Jerry Moran—all of whom
raised their own objections to the BCRA and

---

[1] After the American Healthcare Act (AHCA) was shot down by
voters, Republicans zombified the bill and gave it a new name.

37

refused to support it—the bill is now headed for the trash bin.

Watching McConnell choke is the cathartic victory that many have been yearning for. But the movement to torpedo the BCRA wasn't exclusively comprised of bitter liberals. This was a *massively* unpopular bill that earned derision from Democrats, Independents, and Republicans alike. Democratic lawmakers may have amplified the movement to stop the bill, but the lion's share of credit for flooding congressional offices with phone calls and causing chaos at GOP Senators' recent town hall events belongs to the American people who were able to put aside their differences and unite behind one imperative—defeating a reprehensible piece of legislation that would have blackballed more than 22 million people from the health insurance market.

Take a minute to consider how big this is.

Ever since Donald Trump took the Oath of Office back in January, America has felt less like a union and more like a powder keg splattered with gasoline. The rancid aftertaste of the 2016 election still lingers. You don't have to look hard to find aggrieved Hillary Clinton voters pontificating about Russian agents tampering with voting machines[2] and throwing around words like "traitor" with alarming abandon. This paranoid jingoism is just as palpable in President Trump's self-victimizing Tweets and his followers' rumblings about a deep state plot against their dear leader. When partisanship becomes this dogmatic and hysterical, there's no limit to how each side can dismiss or manipulate facts to serve its own narrative of what is real, what is happening, and *why* it's happening.

And yet, somehow, the cold, hard truth about what the BCRA would have done to millions of Americans managed to rise above the fray. It probably helped that the bill's most noxious parts—particularly, the Medicaid cuts and the repeal of protections for people with pre-existing conditions—were explicitly spelled out and written into a U.S. government document that anyone can Google and read for themselves. But the toxic guts of the BCRA were only revealed to the public a few weeks ago, which brings us to the more likely explanation for why the American people came

---

[2] This is *extremely* different from the far more likely charge of economic collusion between the Trump campaign and Russia.

together to stop this bill.

It's quite simple.

Most of us don't want to die, and we also don't want to be strong-armed into paying top dollar for shitty health insurance. (If the growing support for an American single-payer health care system is any evidence, one could reasonably argue that most Americans would prefer to avoid the headache of health insurance altogether.) On this elemental issue, the American people have finally found a few inches of common ground.

If you feel like celebrating, go ahead: Take your shoes off, throw on a Prince record, and party like it's 2017.[3] What happened to the BCRA is a testament to the ecstatic power of grassroots organization, human empathy, and the fleeting manner in which bipartisanship sometimes *works*. The American people have won an important and historic battle. But our work has just begun. With the BCRA dead in the water, there's now an even greater challenge fast-approaching on the horizon—fixing America's expensive, ineffective,

---

[3] If you're thinking, "This is *way* too specific to be rhetorical," you're right. This is exactly how I reacted to the BCRA defeat.

and cruel health care system.[4]

The shared dream of living long and simplifying the way that healthcare is delivered is the most important thing for everyone who helped kill the BCRA to focus on now. It is the one shared goal that may yet prevent liberals from relapsing into loyal apologists for the important yet deeply flawed Affordable Care Act. Keeping this dream alive will put the Republican leaders who crafted the BCRA in the uncomfortable position of knowing that a significant number of conservative voters are no longer buying what McConnell and Co. are peddling. After nearly a decade of promising voters a fix for the ACA's high deductibles and paltry provider networks, House and Senate Republicans delivered a bill that would have *worsened* nearly everything that most people hate about health insurance.

Their failure is our calling to envision something better and unite behind it.

---

[4] Some context for the use of "cruel" here. A study by *Social Science & Medicine* journal found that 90% of crowdfunding campaigns for medical patients—of which there are tens of thousands—fail to reach their financial goal.

The discreet hypocrisy
of the bourgeoisie

SEPTEMBER 20, 2017

Of course Harvard changed its mind about giving
Chelsea Manning an academic fellowship.[1] Are we
really going to pretend that this about-face by the
most piously revered university in the Ivy
League—let alone the United States—is shocking?
The only thing about this turn of events that's
truly surprising is the fact that Manning's
invitation managed to get past Harvard's
administrative gatekeepers and go public before
someone at the top frantically issued a recall.

Dean Douglas W. Elmendorf wasn't kidding
when he said that offering Manning a fellowship at
Harvard Kennedy School was "a mistake."
Extending an offer like this to a former soldier

---

[1] For those who missed this story, Harvard offered Chelsea
Manning an academic fellowship, only to revoke it days later.
The fellows whose invitations weren't rescinded by the Harvard
administration included Sean Spicer and Corey Lewandowski.

who broke military protocol in order to shine light on war crimes—and did jail time for it—is an affront to one of the most intrinsic traditions of Harvard: Respecting and protecting today's societal hierarchies, their masters, and their rules.

A few decades before Manning was deployed to Iraq, one of Harvard's favorite graduates leaked a continuous stream of government secrets. That leaker was Henry Kissinger. The year was 1968 and President Johnson was engaged in a series of peace talks to end the Vietnam War. These talks offered hope to millions of Americans and Vietnamese, but for Richard Nixon—then a candidate—ending the war would have undermined his presidential campaign.[2] So the politically ambitious Kissinger created an intel backchannel between himself and the Nixon campaign. For months, Kissinger fed classified information about the peace talks to Nixon's team. This information was ultimately used to sabotage the talks, secure Nixon's victory, and prolong the Vietnam War.

---

[2] Nixon argued that pulling U.S. troops out of the war in Vietnam would have been disastrous: That it was better to keep fighting and achieve "peace with honor" in Vietnam.

Kissinger was never punished for leaking state secrets. Granted, it took some time for his crime to be uncovered by historians. But the eventual revelation didn't stop Kissinger from enjoying a fabulous political career and a retirement rich with international awards, think tank appointments, and regular speaking engagements at institutions like Harvard. What absolved Kissinger from the textbook punishment for leaking classified intel—the same thing for which Manning was imprisoned and tortured[3]—was Kissinger's privilege as an Ivy League-educated adviser to the president. As countless studies, books and criminal cases have shown us, the rule of U.S. law is applied far more severely to those at the bottom of our socioeconomic ladder than to those who manage to ascend its highest rungs. If Kissinger's career isn't enough to demonstrate this, look no further than prolific contractor stiffer and self-described sexual predator Donald Trump, who above all legal odds managed to stay rich and occupy the same White House in which Kissinger once held court.

---

[3] Chelsea Manning was kept in solitary confinement for *nearly a year*. She was stripped naked at night and at times, guards took away her eyeglasses, leaving her more or less blind. The UN special rapporteur on torture, Juan Mendez, condemned this.

The logical question to ask, in the wake of Harvard revoking Manning's fellowship, is why this appraisal of character and conduct was not applied to Kissinger. But of course, the question sounds laughably naive because most of us understand the answer on a subconscious level. Manning broke the cardinal rule that Kissinger played by and Harvard has upheld — don't upset the established order that runs the world. When viewed from a distance, Kissinger's treachery against President Johnson fits comfortably within the great American tradition of imperial warfare. It may have been insubordinate, but it did nothing to endanger the ambitions and power of America's military-industrial captains. Manning threatened to disempower those captains and their hierarchy by showing the world how unrestrained military power can defile and destroy innocent people.

One of the illustrious men whom Manning threatened was former CIA director and Harvard senior fellow Michael Morell, who resigned from his Harvard Kennedy School post as soon as Manning was offered a fellowship. During his time at the CIA, Morell approved indiscriminate drone strikes and called for bringing back the 9/11 era torture of prisoners. Both of those acts would constitute violations of international law, but that hasn't stopped Morell from defending his tenure, and it didn't stop Harvard from offering him his own campus office. The same provision applies to former Harvard lecturer and retired four-star Gen. David Petraeus, another classified intelligence leaker whose sole motivation appears to have been sex with his biographer, Paula Broadwell.

All of this—the hypocrisy, the double standard for elites, and the role that Harvard has played again and again in propagating both—demands a thorough scrutinizing of the conventional premise that America's top university is the mecca of inquiry and progress. There is nothing progressive about coddling America's masters and commanders from the consequences of their most unlawful and unethical actions.

As we are reminded by the presidency of Donald Trump and the alarming events that have taken place since he took the oath of office[4], very bad things can happen when the people in charge are not held accountable by institutions. There is

---

[4] Example: During Trump's first year as president, U.S. military forces were estimated to have killed more civilians in the Middle East than the Obama administration did *over eight years.*

no academic institution more capable of holding powerful yet morally bankrupt men accountable than Harvard. That Harvard has instead showered these men with academic prestige is one of the greatest failures of our higher education system. It might be hard to grasp this when you're strolling across The Quad or trying on crimson sweaters at the Coop, but the Harvard tradition of propping up elites can have horrifying consequences for regular people. When the Vietnam peace talks failed—thanks in large part to Henry Kissinger's betrayal—the war raged on for years. Tens of thousands of people were killed. Why? So that one ambitious little man could climb to the top of his profession and stand tall as a global leader.

The Harvard dream.

Imagine something better

SEPTEMBER 25, 2017

Imagination is the most underappreciated weapon in mankind's toolbox. It can spark groundswells of popular advocacy and resistance. It can lay the foundations for an entire generation's worth of political development and progress. Dr. Martin Luther King Jr.'s civil rights movement, FDR's New Deal, and Lincoln's Emancipation Proclamation are epic testaments to the power of collective imagination—of redefining what's possible and pragmatic.

Today, after a hurricane powerful enough to register on seismographs thrashed the coasts of Puerto Rico and Florida, as wildfires incinerate the hills of the American West, and as institutionalized inequality mercilessly dictates who survives these climate disasters and who is left to die, we are charged once again with re-evaluating our options. In spite of Donald Trump and the septic stew of

"America first" beliefs that his presidency has emboldened, most of the world has arrived at a consensus that the warming of our oceans and our atmosphere—climate change—has made it easier for destructive weather events to mutate from textbook maladies into meteorological monsters with no precedent. Most scientists and civilians now agree that there is a tangible line between global warming and the carbon emissions that are unleashed wherever we burn fossil fuels like petroleum and coal. And as many of us cognitively recognize, the victims of global warming are almost uniformly those who can't afford luxuries like an emergency plane ticket to safety or regular access to food, shelter and medicine.

The diagnosis for surviving this new and dangerous world is both simple and damning.

We need to imagine a better one. Right now.

It might seem strange to devote an entire essay to such an obvious conclusion. But America is experiencing a strange chapter of history in which common sense is dangerously vulnerable to partisanship. I refer not only to the modern Republican Party—a cabal of immovable climate change denialists which Noam Chomsky rightly called the "most dangerous organization on earth"—but also the once-bold Democratic Party, which has embraced the sucker's conclusion that "pragmatism" means not rocking the boat too much. Even as the Democrats trepidatiously move to the left of Hillary Clinton's centrist campaign failure with economic proposals like the "Better Deal" and Bernie Sanders' single-payer health care bill, the issue of climate change has yet to catch fire in a game-changing, galvanizing way. The solutions that we are offered—buy LED light bulbs, buy solar panels, buy a composting bin, buy an electric car—are mostly individualistic. It's a sort of green self-betterment program in which the burden of fighting climate change is placed on regular people, as opposed to the industries, entities, and structures of commerce that have largely created this environmental crisis.

As an exercise, consider these questions. What if U.S. lawmakers stopped handing out subsidies to fossil fuel harvesters? What if, instead, some of these subsidies were diverted towards installing solar panels on every home in America? What might that world look like? This is far from a complete solution to climate change, of course.

Rather, in the context of climate disasters such as Hurricane Irma, these are practical questions to be asking. But at this moment in America, they are audacious and even ludicrous questions because they don't compute with the neoliberal "free market" ideology that has shaped our economy for the past four decades. These questions are an affront to the lingering idea that there's no such thing as a free lunch—that a person is only as good as their labor and their account balance. *Free solar panels for everyone?! We're just gonna start handing them out like candy? We can't possibly do that!*

Except that we can. If we really want to.

Ideologies can die more easily than we think. They can take root for centuries only to be chopped down with a few years of organizing and intention. It took Emmeline Pankhurst and the suffragette movement slightly more than a decade to force the British government to allow women the right to vote. It took just as long for a majority of Americans—including the president—to embrace a crazy idea that Henry Ford had been talking about and offering his factory workers for several years: the weekend.

Time and again, societies have turned pie-in-the-sky fantasies into new realities when circumstance necessitates a new course. The climate crises that we have just witnessed are a loud and unignorable calling for all of us to use our imaginations once again. Whether the green future is less capitalistic (a solid bet, given Millennials' growing disenchantment with the market), more technologically sophisticated, some combination of the two, or something we haven't thought of yet, we *must* kickstart the process of envisioning our next chapter. How? By accepting the hard truth that the world we've considered normal and permanent for most of our lives is reaching its expiration date. Systemic tweaks and incremental steps will no longer be enough.

The center will not hold.

Our crisis of empathy

OCTOBER 4, 2017

As millions of Americans took to social media last night to contemplate the horror of the Las Vegas massacre—the deadliest mass shooting committed by an individual in U.S. history—a tweet from one of the artists playing at the ill-fated music festival stood out.

Caleb Keeter, a guitarist for Josh Abbott Band, announced that he had changed his mind about gun control and would begin fighting for firearm restrictions. Surviving the shooting and seeing the gruesome damage inflicted upon the audience by hail after hail of bullets was enough for Keeter to renounce his long-held reverence for the Second Amendment. "I cannot express how wrong I was," Keeter wrote. "Enough is enough."

A short time later, media outlets picked up the story and it went viral. It's easy to understand why.

In times like these, when everything seems to be going off the rails and there's literally blood running in the streets, you look for hope wherever you can find it. For the considerable majority of Americans who support firearm ownership restrictions, Keeter's change of heart on gun rights was a huge deal. If a celebrity from the country music circuit—not exactly a bastion of liberal ideology—is willing to re-evaluate America's lack of gun laws, something *has* to change soon, right?

I'm not so sure.

While I commend Keeter for having the humility to admit that his former beliefs may have been misguided, I'm reluctant to read his words as a profound turn in the road towards a less violent and bullet-riddled America.

What Keeter is doing here fits within an unfortunate history of Americans abandoning an ideology only after they've experienced its most destructive consequences. You don't have to reach far back in time to find public instances of this.

Remember that guy who showed up at Paul Ryan's town hall earlier this year and told him not to repeal the Affordable Care Act? His name is Jeff Jeans, an entrepreneur who hated and opposed the ACA until the day he was diagnosed with cancer.

If you've been watching the news lately, you'll recall that New England Patriots owner Bob Kraft criticized Donald Trump for trying to punish the NFL players who chose to kneel during the National Anthem. And yet, Trump's penchant for suppressing free speech at his rallies wasn't enough to stop Kraft from supporting Trump on the campaign trail and in the months that followed his electoral victory. The grim reality of Trump's penchant only set in when Kraft's own employees suddenly became the president's latest target.

Proximal empathy—the sort that one develops after they or someone close to them experiences something bad—might be enough to prevent a one-off disaster. But it's not nearly enough to fertilize a just and peaceful society. Empathy, in its truest form, should never be proximal. It should be a basic foundation upon which an individual (or the state) makes decisions that will affect others. The big question that should inform the decision maker is, "Will this cause pain and suffering for other people? Directly *or* indirectly?" The answer to that question shouldn't necessarily determine what course of action the individual takes, but it should be a constant and profound consideration.

As a nation, America appears to have lost this critical base layer of empathy. The concrete steps that could be taken towards addressing some of our worst afflictions—medical debt and access to health care, systemic poverty, racial oppression, and gun violence—are not taken because too many people with power routinely choose the opposite approach: to let those afflictions go untreated and ignore the consequential pain and suffering.

In this country, people are shot every week because too many Americans have decided that their right to own guns is worth the great danger that this poses to all Americans. Many of the victims left disfigured and disabled by those shootings are then faced with enormous hospital bills and the threat of medical bankruptcy because too many Americans have decided that access to healthcare is not a human right, but a privilege for those who work the hardest and maintain a robust checking account. (The logic here is self-fulfilling: If you can afford to oppose universal health care, that means you're a virtuous worker.)

This past summer, I encountered a young mother and her daughter in the parking lot of a supermarket. Quietly and calmly, the mother explained to me that her daughter, Adrianne, was suffering from brain cancer. She handed me an index card with a URL scribbled on it. This was the link to Adrianne's GoFundMe campaign—an online fundraiser to cover her medical bills. That night, I went online and made a small donation, but I felt nauseous knowing that for Adrianne's family and so many others, the whims of random strangers with money were the last safety net preventing them from falling into the abyss.

At this very moment, a GoFundMe campaign for the victims of the Las Vegas massacre has amassed several million dollars in donations.[1] That alone should be the alarm bell that something has gone horribly wrong here—that even something as cataclysmic as a mass shooting isn't enough to inspire more empathy from the state and its core supporters—but this happens after almost every mass shooting. Upholding human life and dignity

---

[1] The money raised by the GoFundMe account only went so far. Less than one month after the Las Vegas shooting, CNN reported that many of the injured survivors were struggling to pay their medical bills.

is reduced to an act of crowdfunded charity. Anything more civic and compassionate would offend the sensibilities of those who want America to be Spartan and unyielding.

If we truly want to be the kind of country in which peace and prosperity for all are bedrock, we need to learn how to feel empathy for those whose pain we don't personally experience. Some of us are there already. Many are just showing up. The Caleb Keeters, Jeff Jeanses, and Bob Krafts of the world can still play a crucial role as advocates for empathy that is foundational, renewing, and lasting. The ultimate test will be whether these folks can apply their circumstantial empathy to broader intersectional struggles that involve human suffering.

Until then, watch your back.

And save your money.

The most popular man
in Massachusetts

DECEMBER 6, 2017

In case you haven't heard, Charlie Baker is really popular.[1]

This data-driven fact is regularly trotted out by both conservative and liberal media outlets as if it were the most illustrious thing that an elected official can strive for—not legislative accomplishments, not courage, but simply being liked by as many people as possible.

Baker, who recently announced his re-election bid, certainly fits this profile. As a governor, he has been nothing but cautious about upsetting anyone. For this alone, most Massachusetts residents like him and are ready to vote for him again.

---

[1] Charlie Baker, the "moderate" Republican governor of Massachusetts, has been regularly ranked as the most popular governor in America.

Confused? Me too.

Before the Trump era, Baker's approval
numbers would have made sense. He ran as a
moderate Republican who would reduce spending
but keep the peace with Massachusetts liberals.
That's pretty much how his first term has played
out. We were reminded of Baker's conservative
foundation when he called for Medicaid cuts and
refused to support the so-called millionaires' tax.
But his reluctance to pursue those agenda items
full steam is a reminder that Baker knows he's on a
short leash. Maybe that's why so many liberals like
him. Baker is keenly aware that the majority of
Massachusetts swings further left than he does. He
knows that liberals could push him out of office if
he wanders too far to the right. He listens to them
and acts accordingly.

Or so it appears.

Let's take a closer look at what has actually
happened since Massachusetts joined the U.S.
Climate Alliance[2] after President Trump pulled the

---

[2] The U.S. Climate Alliance is a coalition of states dedicated to
reducing greenhouse emissions cooperatively. It's basically a
giant "fuck you" to Donald Trump and the federal government.
California and New York were among the founding states.

U.S. out of the Paris climate accord. Many Massachusetts liberals celebrated the move as evidence of Baker's practicality. But what most still haven't acknowledged is the inconvenient truth that Baker has barely committed Massachusetts to transitioning to clean energy alternatives, as required of all states that join the U.S. Climate Alliance. (He hasn't said much about the slate of proposed fossil fuel projects in Massachusetts either.) This pattern of placation and inaction also reveals itself when we reconcile Baker's criticisms of the Trump administration's draconian language on immigration with the fact that Baker has stood by and done nothing as emboldened ICE agents terrorize the state's communities and rip Massachusetts families apart. Even Baker's much-publicized refusal to vote for either of the two presidential candidates in the 2016 election feels like a cheap stunt when one considers the weight and consequence of that election.

Massachusetts has the precedent, the potential, and the *responsibility* to be a leading state in the struggle to defend policies on climate, healthcare, and fair tax codes. Our legacy suggests that the commonwealth should be standing with states like California, New York, and Washington as they pass their own climate change laws, affordable health care expansions, and public college plans.

But we're not. Because we've lowered the bar for what the governor must do.

When it comes to legislation, the governor doesn't have that much leverage other than coaxing or cajoling local lawmakers to support their agenda. But in setting and articulating that agenda, the governor actually has a tremendous amount of power. The governor gets to redefine what's possible and necessary on a massive public scale. As the tech industry crowd might say, the governor is a democratically-elected "thought leader[3]" with a mandate to push the state government in a certain direction, so long as they doesn't abandon their core campaign promises.

As a Massachusetts resident proud to hail from the state whose past governors have led the nation on issues like health care access, same-sex marriage, and progressive taxation, Baker's popularity not only mystifies me—it alarms me. It suggests that a historically bold and visionary state

---

[3] I absolutely loathe the term "thought leader," but it's a fairly accurate way to describe the role of governor and its power.

is now surrendering its moxie and principles to the convenience of relativism in the age of Trump. We are deceiving ourselves with the notion that the governor's office is insignificant enough to be occupied by a man who lacks vision and bravery.

Charlie Baker does not deserve a second term in office. Being cautious in the era of Trump and an extremist Republican Party is neither courageous nor practical. It's a form of distant and cowardly collaboration that ultimately enables the most rabidly partisan lawmakers to do their worst. It's essentially saying to Trump and his Congressional butler boys, "I don't *like* what you're doing, but goddamnit, I'll still work with you." We are living in a moment when our economic opportunities, our access to medical care, our environment, and our civil liberties are threatened each week. And the best that "America's most popular governor" can do is make insincere and often vacuous gestures that do little but appease those voters who
pine for the days of reasonable bipartisanship.

Massachusetts can do better. We *have* done better.

Why stop now?

Cobalt Thorium GOP

DECEMBER 2, 2017

America runs on taxation.

This is something that bears repeating in a country where taxes — the money that each of us puts into the "Keep America's Lights On" jar — are a casually reviled concept. In America, there is an entire industry built on helping people avoid giving money to Uncle Sam. The most recent United States presidents have cut taxes in some way. The Republican Party, which accounts for more than one quarter of the American electorate, has fashioned itself into an extremist organization that believes in "starving" the government by relieving oligarchs of their civic burden.

And yet, in spite of all this, we've never experienced a moment when America's lights have gone out — when tax revenues plummet to such a low point that the government has no choice but to shut down programs and services that are integral to everyday American life.

This is not to suggest that America isn't already suffering from fiscal duress. We are, and it's getting worse. But even as wages stagnate, living costs soar, and services like Medicaid and CHIP[1] face budget crises, we have to recognize that these services still *exist.* Each day, millions of people living on the fringes of our economy manage to find their way through the red tape to welfare programs that their tax dollars pay for. Even those who have the privilege of buying groceries from Whole Foods and enrolling in a PPO plan stand to benefit from taxpayer-subsidized utilities like emergency services and environmental protection agencies.

It is assumed that these utilities will always be there for us whenever we need them. And that is what allows civil society to sustain itself in America. Public utilities are the fence between a relatively peaceful society and a Hobbesian

---

[1] CHIP stands for Children's Health Insurance Program. As of today, its funding has lapsed, and Congress has done nothing

wilderness where starvation, violence, disease, and desperation are defining features of the landscape. This is why no American president or Congress has gone and torn down the fence that our taxes built. To fantasize about bleeding the government dry is very different from actually doing it. The societal consequences would be unimaginable. So we don't imagine them. We dream about never having to file a tax return again, and how great it would feel. And that's it.

America's tax resentment runs no deeper.

It was this kind of entrenched thinking that gave George W. Bush and Republican lawmakers the confidence and political capital to cut taxes in 2002, with most of the cuts going to corporations and the wealthy. (They were later extended by Barack Obama.) These cuts were tough on America's public programs, but not a death sentence. For most Americans, this was a good thing. For Republican Party leaders and their most powerful donors, it was a missed opportunity to claw back even more cash from the public coffers.

This would become the party's governing mission for the next eight years.

Today, nearly a decade after W hung up his dinner jacket and returned to Texas to paint dogs and veterans for the rest of his life, the Republican Senate has released and *passed* its master plan to expand the Bush tax cuts that went to America's highest earners. It is a breathtaking piece of legislation. Reckless. Sloppy. And completely devoid of empathy for the billions of people whose lives will be negatively impacted.

Here is what you — an ordinary American — can expect if the Republican tax bill that the Senate just passed is signed into law by Donald Trump.

Nothing.

The only tax cut you will receive as a middle or working class citizen will be temporary. When it expires, your tax rates will go back up and you'll be left alone to shoulder that burden. The tax reform will almost certainly not spark a hiring boom in the private sector — this has *never* happened in the wake of tax cuts, despite Republicans' empty promises that it would — so if you're jobless or if you get laid off, you'll have to take your chances in the same shitty labor market we now face. Actually, the market will probably get *worse* because the tax plan will be brutal for small businesses and force a lot of them to downsize or shutter.

Worse yet, the tax dollars of ordinary working Americans alone won't be enough to sustain the public resources that make life less dangerous for those who are struggling. There will be virtually no food or housing assistance to fall back on if your job applications go nowhere or if your savings run out. Medicare and Medicaid will be defunded and your insurance options will become vastly more expensive because the Republican tax bill also kills the Affordable Care Act mandate that requires everyone to have health insurance. Even the money that *you paid into* Social Security will be used to offset the cost of making sure that the wealthy and their progeny don't have to pay a penny more in taxes.

If you decide to improve your own income prospects by going to school for an advanced degree, you'd better have a lot of cash squirreled away because nothing will be done to stem the already insane cost[2] of undergraduate tuition. And for all you older kids, any tuition assistance you receive for a grad program will be taxed as *income*. Get used to news like this because under the GOP tax bill, if you're not rich, you'll have to cough up more cash for nearly everything—including things that your taxes subsidize right now. Even if you hit rock bottom and decide that your best option is to drive to the nearest national park and begin a new life as a Hugh Glass-esque hermit[3], living off the land and forsaking what's left of society, you should know in advance that you will have to pay a significantly heftier price just to be allowed into the park, and of course, you'll have to pay the fee again every time you re-enter.

---

[2] Fun fact: the average American high school senior now spends nearly $1,700 on college applications. Not tuition: *applications.*

[3] Hugh Glass was the fur trapper and bear mauling survivor whom Leonardo DiCaprio portrayed in *The Revenant.*

Never forget—you will suffer all of this so that rich people and corporations will be relieved of paying higher taxes. Permanently.

If there's any single piece of this misanthropic and nihilistic bill that we should pay special attention to, it's the temporary tax cut for the middle and working classes, which the Republicans are spotlighting to persuade regular people that tax reform will be good for them. Some economists and pundits have compared this fleeting tax cut to the carrot that a wagon driver would dangle in front of a horse. In fact, it's worse. The carrot was dangled out of the horse's reach — creating an eternal chase for a prize that the horse can never have. But the Republican tax scam strategy amounts to letting the horse eat the carrot immediately. Once the carrot is gone, that's it. The horse is stuck pulling the wagon for the rest of eternity, left with nothing but the bitter memory of how sweet that one carrot tasted.

The cruelty of this strategy is breathtaking. But what's just as urgent to consider as the Republicans send their tax reform bill back to the House is how incredibly dangerous it would be to do something like this to an entire country of people who are *already* highly anxious about their economic prospects. It is well established in the fields of mental health that having a good thing ripped away from you without warning is far more traumatic and damaging than never having the thing at all. The Republican tax bill would offer billions of cash-strapped people a glimmer of hope that would suddenly vanish, along with most of the public utilities that keep the most vulnerable from drowning. When that happens, America will become a very dark place. The question that most will be left wondering as the country rips itself apart is, "*What the fuck just happened?!*" Meanwhile, the lucky beneficiaries of the tax reform bill will weather the storm in their gated communities and mountaintop bug-out bunkers[4]. And when the smoke finally clears, America will cease to be the sort of nation that inspires hope.

---

[4] This is neither humor nor hyperbole. The wealthy are preparing for doomsday events. There are many stories exploring this trend, and according to most, high-security bunkers are all the rage for the Elon Musks of the world.

Instead, it will become the ultimate cautionary tale of what happens when a society gives up on the idea of common good.

This fate is almost too grim to consider, and that's the problem. People don't like to spend their waking hours thinking about the worst that could happen. We saw this in the years that preceded entirely predictable disasters like the 2007 housing market crash, or the election of Donald Trump. There was smoke on the horizon and most of us ignored it. But even when disaster arrives at your doorstep, accepting its presence can be too much for the average person. Just a few days after Trump won the presidency, the great Russian journalist and Putin expert Masha Gessen wrote an article called "Rules For Autocracy" that contained an important yet overlooked point for Americans reeling from the 2016 election. When your world and way of life are suddenly in danger, talking about that danger honestly and openly with your friends can put you at risk of sounding like the crazy person in the room. That's a deeply embarrassing position to be in, at best, and it can leave you feeling isolated, powerless, and skeptical of your own sanity — even if there's more than enough evidence to corroborate your hunch that things are about to get very bad.

But there are exceptions.

Earlier this year, millions of Americans rose up and defeated the Republican Party's effort to take affordable healthcare away from people with modest income and pre-existing conditions. The folks who led this grassroots resistance faced the most nightmarish consequences of cutting down healthcare. They absorbed the reality this would kill people. They fought back furiously, calling their Senators and assailing them at town halls, and they won.

So where are these folks now? Is America too emotionally fatigued to stop the Republican Party's apocalyptic tax reform bill? Is the concept of tax reform too wonky to catch fire and inspire grassroots resistance like healthcare repeal did? Or is the scorched earth devastation of the tax bill too detached from our relatively stable present? Even in their ugliest form, neither of the Republicans' healthcare repeal bills ever threatened to defund

America's public infrastructure like the tax bill would. And even on our most contempt-ridden days of tax season, most of us have never truly tinkered with the Pandora's Box of questions that are unique to this chapter of US history.

What would happen if we just stopped investing in civil society?

Or believing in it?

We no longer have the luxury of flirting with this question. We must engage with it today, as though our lives depended on it. (Because they do.) Until then, we will remain caught in vicious war between slashing taxes and keeping America's lights on. It is a war that the Republican Party and its donors are now within reach of winning, and there might not be any coming back from that resolution. If they win, most of us will feel the impact. Many will swear that they never saw it coming. But those of us who did recognize this tax reform bill as a nuclear time bomb will be forever haunted by what might have happened if more people had cared —or if we had been given just a little more time to raise the alarm and stop the bomb from going off. And that is the single most important thing that every one of us needs to understand right now.

We don't have much time.

The Jones Window

DECEMBER 13, 2017

He did it.

Doug Jones, a civil rights attorney[1] and a Democrat, is going to fill Jeff Sessions' vacant Alabama Senate seat.

After a nailbiter race against Republican Roy Moore—a bigot, a revisionist historian[2], and, according to nine women, a sexual predator—Jones won the special election by a razor-thin margin. Better-than-expected turnout from black voters, particularly in cities like Montgomery, appears to have handed the race to Jones. Again, just because this merits remarking upon, an Alabama Democrat is headed to

---

[1] This is putting it rather lightly. Doug Jones literally prosecuted the Ku Klux Klan members who murdered four black girls by throwing a bomb into a Birmingham church in 1963.

[2] At one point in the race, Moore harkened back to the era of slavery as a better time for Americans.

Washington to take over Jeff Sessions' Senate seat.

This is really happening.

It wasn't supposed to.

In the last 60 years, Alabama has thrown its support behind only one Democratic presidential nominee. Its most recent Democratic senator, Richard Shelby, migrated over to the Republican Party more than two decades ago. He's still in office, but now he'll be joined by a guy who wants to bring renewable energy, a higher minimum wage, and criminal justice reform to the Yellowhammer State. On a national scale, the GOP Congress will now have an even thinner margin for passing its tax bill[3], and any sort of legislation that materializes next year. This is a Senate shakeup that will have significant and lasting consequences for America as a whole.

Just a few months ago, the thought of someone like Jones tipping the balance in a historically crimson state was unthinkable. So what triggered

---

[3] The Republicans didn't wait for Jones to be seated. They voted on the tax bill with Luther Strange—the unelected Republican seat warmer— filling in for Jones. The bill passed. Dick move.

this seismic moment in U.S. history? The exit polls will paint a more vivid picture in the week ahead[4]. But between looking back at the months that led up to the race and reviewing the dispatches from various Alabama precincts, it's already clear that Tuesday's election came down to not only strong voter turnout, but a different and uncharted political era with new rules, new challenges, and new opportunities for underdogs.

Let's start with Roy Moore himself.

To liberals, moderates and some conservatives, the GOP contender was an absurdist manifestation of Republican Party sentiments: a race-baiting, LGBT-hating, 19th Amendment-shredding caricature. Jeff Sessions on steroids, basically. Throw in several credible allegations of cruising underage girls at the local mall and you've got a candidate so grotesque that his shot at victory would have been laughable before Donald Trump rose to power. And that's what squelched any ounce of morbid comedy from the race—knowing that in Trump's Republican Party, there is a special place for a man like Roy Moore. As Alabama

---

[4] It's official now: black voters boosted Doug Jones to victory.

Governor Kay Ivey put it shortly before the election, "We need to have a Republican in the United States Senate to vote on things."

What's remarkable about Ivey's rationale for holding her nose firmly and supporting Roy Moore—echoed by many other Alabama GOP officials—is how naked it is. The usual varnish about state rights, middle-class jobs, or religious freedom is missing. Ivey plainly stated that she would vote for Moore to further consolidate the Republican Party's grip on America. This signifies a party so obsessed with power and emboldened by its electoral gains that its representatives aren't even *pretending* to care about bipartisanship or prosperity for the common person. The modern Republican Party has affirmed that it's now willing to do anything it takes to fill seats and score more legislative "wins." After amassing behind Trump and especially after falling in line for Moore, the party now resembles a consequentialist cult in which the end justifies any means.

This is an enormous gift to the Democratic Party. Why? Because since 2016, the Republicans' legislative agenda has proven nationally unpopular enough that the party's kamikaze determination to ram that agenda through Congress—even if it means propping up a monster like Roy Moore—is starting to feel like an aggressive takeover to millions of working Americans who don't want to lose their health coverage or their tax benefits. When Trump and Clinton locked horns last year, losing either of those things wasn't conceivable enough to compel preventative voting. Today, both possibilities are right at our door. A handful of Republicans in Washington have the power to decide if those possibilities will come to pass.

Americans who oppose the GOP agenda understand this.

They are acting.

We saw their cognitive urgency during the blitz of phone calls and town hall demonstrations that ultimately discouraged the GOP from repealing the Affordable Care Act. (Twice!) We felt it more recently during the Virginia elections in which a transgender journalist and a Democratic Socialist were among the winners.

But Tuesday night's Alabama race is a major turning point. It is a loud and decisive repudiation of the Republican Party's cynical scorched earth strategy, in one of the party's stronghold states. It was a confirmation that likely Democratic voters (and more) are angry, anxious, and hopeful enough to vote with renewed diligence. Considering that the full voting might of Doug Jones supporters was almost certainly suppressed due to Alabama's photo ID laws[5], it's thrilling to imagine what the final election results might have looked like had those laws *not* been in place.

That possibility—that opportunity—should occupy the mind of every Democratic candidate, strategist, and voter in the weeks ahead. The Doug Jones victory is a window that will not remain open for long. It is a call for Democrats to compete everywhere. The rules of what's normal in politics are now being hastily rewritten. The bedrock of what's achievable is cracking up every week. The Democrats are not in Kansas anymore.

Starting today, they should change that.

---

[5] Not only does the Alabama legislature require voters to produce a government-issued photo ID, but it has also closed many of the DMVs across the state—mostly in poor black communities. This, in turn, has depressed voter turnout.

Surviving austerity

DECEMBER 20, 2017

The Republicans just passed a tax bill that is going to kill people.

The bill, which sailed through the House and Senate today despite significant opposition from the public, adds a staggering sum to the national debt. The GOP is already planning to pay off that debt by defunding our essential taxpayer-funded safety net programs such as Medicare, Medicaid, and Social Security. Many of the people whose lives depend on those programs are going to die so that rich people, corporations, and many Republican lawmakers can get a big tax break.

This is what will happen if we do nothing.

Even as America's social infrastructure hangs in the balance, it's important to remember that we still have a chance to avert the worst repercussions of the tax bill. Next year's midterm elections, which take place on November 6th, are the ultimate do-or-die moment for repudiating the brazenly undemocratic manner in which the GOP assembled and ratified this bill: with barely any regard for public sentiment or consequence. Those elections are an opportunity to re-stack Congress with principled legislators who will do everything they can to recapture the windfall of this wealth transfer for the benefit of the public.

But first, we have to *make it* to next November.

If the Republicans manage to begin draining our social utilities between now and then — which they almost certainly will — then it's safe to say that 2018 is going to be one of the toughest years that many of us will ever experience.

America is heading straight into the cold and brutal territory of austerity.

So today, as we approach Christmas—a holiday that celebrates generosity, kinship, and love—I write this column (my last of 2017) to propose something. A new and informal social contract to be upheld by those with means, and those without.

Allow me to explain.

One of the oldest taboos in American life is talking openly about money. This kind of fiscal self-censorship transcends class and age. My friends and I—mostly Millennials—will often joke that in 2017, it's much easier to talk about your kinkiest sex fantasies than your checking account balance. This taboo lingers because in American life, wealth conveys not just success, but character. Conventional logic dictates that if you've got lots of money in the bank, you've clearly worked hard, made smart decisions in life, and proven yourself a virtuous, enterprising American.

This mythology is part and parcel with the Republican tax bill, which lavishes money on the "virtuous" while punishing nearly everyone else. Look no further than Senator Chuck Grassley's recent insinuation that those with next to nothing in their pockets must be "spending every damn penny they have...on booze or women or movies."[1]

---

[1] In case this book makes it into the Library of Congress, let me go on the record and say something here: *fuck Chuck Grassley*.

This comment illustrates why so many Americans can't bring themselves to speak candidly about financial hardship they've endured: even if that hardship is the result of random misfortune or something more nefarious like wage-theft. America's current social contract draws barely any distinction between laziness and rotten luck.

If you've lived fairly comfortably these past few years — if you've seldom had to sweat the matter of money — I guarantee you that *at least* three people in your life are privately suffering. These could be people whose occupations might suggest a cushy and steady life. How do I know this? Because I've been one of those people. My byline may appear with recognized outlets like Boston's NPR station, but during the past five years as a writer, I've been on Medicaid twice and endured months with little to no income. I used to avoid revealing any of this because I worried it would terminally compromise the upstanding professional and personal image (or "brand") that I was trying to cultivate.

But what finally encouraged me to become more transparent about my victories *and* my vulnerability was a simple question that I would occasionally get from someone whose relative wealth greatly exceeded mine.

"How are you holding up?"

Consider the wording of that question. There's no presumption of work or enterprise. The key inquiry is humanist. It's a major departure from the way that American often relate to each other — through their occupational endeavors. It's an expression of pure compassion. It is a question that everyone lucky enough to not be gravely imperiled by the incoming wave of GOP-ordered austerity[2] needs to start asking their friends, colleagues, and family members on a regular basis. And those of us who *are* suffering in solitude must find the courage to answer that question honestly. The decades-long code of silence that has erased this kind of discourse from American life must be broken starting now. Because silence during austerity is suicide. Not just for oneself, but for the social fabric of communities. It discourages solidarity and it promotes delusional thinking: it suggests that

---

[2] Paul Ryan, the king of austerity, started teasing Medicare cuts all the way back in January of 2017. A year later, he has all the runway he needs to take off and make these cuts happen.

mettle and grit are all one needs to overcome the immense and systemic dangers that countless Americans will soon find themselves facing.

This weekend, as millions of us celebrate a guy who was born to penniless parents in a loaned manger, take a good, long moment to assess your situation honestly. Decide exactly what you are prepared to ask for, or what you are able to give to others. If a wildfire burned down your house next week, whom could you imagine turning to for shelter and financial assistance? If you're a doctor, what would you be willing to do for a friend whose kid just lost the health insurance they once received through the CHIP program? If a friend of yours came to your door and asked for something to eat[3]—something for their children to eat—what might you say or offer them?

If *you* were that unfortunate, foodless friend, whose door would you knock on?

---

[3] Shortly after writing this column, a dear friend of mine who lives in northern Vermont found himself in this very scenario: a neighbor (with kids) knocked on my friend's door on a snowy night and asked for food. My friend gave the neighbor some of the lamb that he had raised and slaughtered earlier in the year.

Knowing the answers to questions like these is how we make it to next November. Starting today, we must commit to taking care of each other—and ourselves—with renewed urgency and honesty. As long as we do this, we will ensure that the humanity so many honor on December 24th each year prevails through the difficult year ahead and inspires a better kind of American politics.

A kind of politics that dispenses with myth, and lets love in.

Bibliography

Adler, Ben. "Shipping is a big contributor to climate change. So why is it being left out of the Paris deal?" *Grist.* December 5, 2015.

Allison, Tom. *Financial Health of Young America: Measuring Generational Declines between Baby Boomers & Millennials.* Young Invincibles. January 2017.

Andersen, Travis. "State Democrats blast ICE raid targeting sanctuary cities." *Boston Globe.* September 29, 2017.

Bartash, Jeffry. "Here's your meager Social Security cost-of-living adjustment." *MarketWatch.* October 18, 2016.

Belluz, Julia. "The GOP plan for Obamacare could kill more people each year than gun homicides." *Vox.* June 26, 2017.

Berman, Ari. "Alabama, Birthplace of the Voting Rights Act, Is Once Again Gutting Voting Rights." *The Nation.* October 1, 2015.

Bilton, Nick. "Inside The Desperate, Year-Long Hunt To Find Donald Trump's Rumored Apprentice Outtakes." *Vanity Fair.* February 2017.

Bullard, Gabe. "See What Climate Change Means for the World's Poor." *National Geographic.* December 1, 2015.

Bump, Phillip. "Here Is When Each Generation Begins and Ends, According to Facts." *The Atlantic.* March 25, 2014.

Bump, Phillip. "Another day, another poll showing how deeply unpopular the GOP health-care bill is." *Washington Post*. June 22, 2017.

Chandler, Seth. "Tax Cuts In Republican Senate Health Bill Undercut Its Best Justification." *Forbes*. June 26, 2017.

Chesto, Jon. "What's up with the millionaires' tax? Baker isn't saying." *Boston Globe*. June 6, 2017.

Clifford, Catherine. "The real reason for disappearing jobs isn't trade—it's robots." *CNN*. November 21, 2016.

Collins, Chuck. "What Happened to America's Wealth? The Rich Hid It." *Moyers & Company*. July 7, 2017.

Collins, Chuck & Hoxie, Josh. "The GOP Tax Bill Does Nothing to Address Our Racial Wealth Divide." *Institute for Policy Studies*. November 21, 2017.

Cooper, Ryan. "Roy Moore: Lunatic. Bigot. Zealot. Senator?" *The Week*. September 28, 2017.

Davenport, Coral & Lipton, Eric. "Trump Picks Scott Pruitt, Climate Change Denialist, to Lead E.P.A." *New York Times*. December 7, 2016.

Deaton, Jeremy. "Major news networks are failing to explain that Hurricane Harvey was fueled by climate change." *Quartz*. September 9, 2017.

Debot, Brandon, Huang, Chye-Ching, and Marr, Chuck. "ACA Repeal Would Lavish Medicare Tax Cuts on 400 Highest-Income Households." *Center on Budget and Policy Priorities*. January 12, 2017.

Dilanian, Ken. "Former CIA leader defends drone strikes, torture." *Associated Press*. May 4, 2015.

Dooling, Shannon. "While A Chelsea Man Remains In

Immigration Custody, His Family Struggles With A New Normal." *WBUR.* October 19, 2017.

Editorial Board. "511 Days. 555 Mass Shootings. Zero Action from Congress." *New York Times.* November 6, 2017.

Ehrenreich, Barbara. "The US Paradox Of Poverty Is Almost Impossible To Escape." *The Atlantic.* November 29, 2014.

Farrell, John A. "When a Candidate Conspired With a Foreign Power to Win An Election." *Politico.* August 6, 2017.

Faulkner, Tim. "Baker Remains Quiet on Proposed Fossil-Fuel Projects." *ecoRI News.* October 30, 2017.

Franklin, Mary Beth. "Big gap between Social Security cost-of-living adjustment and retiree inflation." *InvestmentNews.* October 24, 2016.

Franta, Benjamin & Supran, Geoffrey. "The fossil fuel industry's invisible colonization of academia." *The Guardian.* March 13, 2017.

Fry, Richard. "Millennials match Baby Boomers as largest generation in U.S. electorate, but will they vote?" *Pew Research Center.* May 16, 2016.

Fuller, Andrea. "Student Debt Payback Far Worse Than Believed." *Wall Street Journal.* January 18, 2017.

Godfrey, Neal. "The Young And The Restless: Millennials On The Move." *Forbes.* October 2, 2016.

Goldman, Adam. "How David Petraeus avoided felony charges and possible prison time." *Washington Post.* January 25, 2016.

Goldstein, Amy. "Cancer survivor who once opposed federal health law challenges Ryan on its repeal." *Washington Post.* January 14, 2017.

Gould, Elise. "2014 Continues a 35-Year Trend of Broad-Based Wage Stagnation." *Economic Policy Institute*. February 19, 2015.

Griffiths, Brent D. "Grassley derides those who spend all their money 'on booze or women or movies.'" *Politico*. December 3, 2017.

Hall, Sam. "The world doesn't need the US to lead climate change action—China will do it instead." *The Telegraph*. May 31, 2017.

Hamblin, James. "A Mandate, in Other Words." *The Atlantic*. March 7, 2017.

Hiltzik, Michael. "Paul Ryan is determined to kill Medicare. This time he might succeed." *Los Angeles Times*. November 23, 2016.

Jenner, Lynn. "Dozens of Wildfires in Western United States." *NASA*. August 28, 2017.

Karni, Annie. "Inside Clinton's GOP recruitment plan." *Politico*. August 9, 2016.

Kaufman, Noah. "Heritage Foundation Gets It Wrong on Costs and Benefits of Climate Action." *World Resources Institute*. March 28, 2017.

Kiley, Jocelyn. "Public support for 'single payer' health coverage grows, driven by Democrats." *Pew Research Center*. June 23, 2017.

Krieg, Gregory. "How Democrats learned to stop worrying and love 'Medicare for all.'" *CNN*. September 12, 2017.

Langille, Sean. "Massachusetts GOP Gov. Charlie Baker: 'Trump made the wrong decision' on DACA." *Washington Examiner*. September 5, 2017.

Levine, Sam. "There Are Huge Obstacles To Casting A Ballot In

Alabama's Special Election." *Huffington Post.* December 11, 2017.

MacAskill, Ewen. "Barack Obama seeks compromise with Republican senators." *The Guardian.* March 14, 2013.

MacAskill, Ewen. "Former CIA leaders go on offensive to deny claim torture was ineffective." *The Guardian.* December 10, 2014.

Mark, Michelle. "How Americans really feel about gun control." *Business Insider.* October 3, 2017.

McCluskey, Priyanka Dayal & O'Sullivan, Jim. "Baker signs 2018 budget, but vetoes $320m in spending." *Boston Globe.* July 17, 2017.

McElwee, Sean. "Are The Democrats Totally Screwed?" *The Outline.* March 9, 2017.

McGrath, Matt. "Trump's 'control-alt-delete' on climate policy." *BBC News.* January 25, 2017.

McLaughlin, Jenna. "If Millennials Had Voted, Last Night Would Have Looked Very Different." *Mother Jones.* November 5, 2014.

Miller, S.A. "Liberals irked by Obama's compromises." *Washington Times.* December 17, 2009.

Murphy, Matt. "Gov. Baker Enters Mass. Into Multi-State Climate Alliance After U.S. Withdraws From Paris Agreement." *State House News Service.* June 2, 2017.

Nelson, Nicole D. "When Will Black Lives Matter in St. Louis?" *New York Times.* September 20, 2017.

Ornstein, Norm. "The Real Story of Obamacare's Birth." *The Atlantic.* July 6, 2015.

Osnos, Evan. "Doomsday Prep for the Super-Rich." *The New*

Yorker. January 30, 2017.

Phillips, Frank. "Environmental groups push to shorten offshore wind timeline." *Boston Globe.* July 7, 2017.

Ponsot, Elisabeth. "These nine women have accused Roy Moore of sexual misconduct." *Quartz.* December 7, 2017.

Reilly, Katie. "What Female Lawmakers Think About the Senate's All-Male Health Care Working Group." *Fortune.* May 8, 2017.

Reilly, Steve. "Hundreds allege Donald Trump doesn't pay his bills." *USA Today.* June 9, 2016.

Salhani, Justin. "Former CIA Director Reveals He Approved Drone Strikes He Knew Would Kill Innocent Children." *ThinkProgress.* November 13, 2015.

Scahill, Jeremy. "The True Scandal Of 2016 Was The Torture Of Chelsea Manning." *The Intercept.* November 8, 2016.

Schumer, Chuck. "A Better Deal for American Workers." *New York Times.* July 24, 2017.

Smith, Austin. "Half of American baby boomers face a frightening retirement reality." *Motley Fool.* December 9, 2016.

Stephenson, Wen. "Houston's Human Catastrophe Started Long Before the Storm." *The Nation.* August 29, 2017.

Strauss, Matthew. "Guitarist Who Performed at Festival in Las Vegas Before Shooting Issues Statement Supporting Gun Control." *Pitchfork.* October 2, 2017.

Taylor, Andrew J. "Millennials Are in a Love Triangle with Capitalism and Socialism." *Foundation for Economic Education.* August 25, 2017.

Terbush, Jon. "Obama is done even pretending to work with

Republicans." *The Week*. February 21, 2014.

Vaidyanathan, Gayathri. "Obama Climate Rules Not Enough to Fight Global Warming." *ClimateWire*. June 3, 2014.

Volcovici, Valerie. "Trump administration tells EPA to cut climate page from website: sources." *Reuters*. January 24, 2017.

Walker, Peter. "Bradley Manning trial: what we know from the leaked WikiLeaks documents." *The Guardian*. July 30, 2013.

Wermund, Benjamin. "Trump's education pick says reform can 'advance God's Kingdom.'" *Politico*. December 2, 2016.

White, Gillian B. "Americans Are Putting Off Medical Treatments Because They Can't Pay." *The Atlantic*. February 9, 2017.

Wilts, Alexandra. "Hurricane Irma has become so strong it's showing up on seismometers used to measure earthquakes." *Independent*. September 5, 2017.

Wolf, Z. Byron. "Roy Moore's incredible 'even though we had slavery' quote." *CNN*. December 8, 2017.

Yglesias, Matthew. "America's Imperial Tradition." *The Atlantic*. October 16, 2006.

Yoder, Steve. "Do Trump Rallies Trample on Protesters' Free Speech?" *The American Prospect*. March 22, 2016.

MILES HOWARD is an author, researcher, and communications consultant whose work has been featured in Southwest: The Magazine, the Boston Phoenix, The Hill, and the Los Angeles Times. His columns appear regularly at WBUR.org. A resident of Jamaica Plain, Miles graduated from the University of Southern California with a degree in English and film. His next book, *Red Sky at Night*, will explore America three years before Trump.

www.ingramcontent.com/pod-product-compliance
Lightning Source LLC
Chambersburg PA
CBHW020511030426
42337CB00011B/336